Charles Janeway Stillé

How a Free People Conduct a Long War

A chapter from English history

Charles Janeway Stillé

How a Free People Conduct a Long War
A chapter from English history

ISBN/EAN: 9783337285975

Printed in Europe, USA, Canada, Australia, Japan

Cover: Foto ©ninafisch / pixelio.de

More available books at **www.hansebooks.com**

HOW A FREE PEOPLE

CONDUCT A LONG WAR:

A

CHAPTER FROM ENGLISH HISTORY

BY

CHARLES J. STILLÉ.

PHILADELPHIA:

COLLINS, PRINTER, 705 JAYNE STREET.

1862.

History, if it be not the merest toy, the idlest pastime of our vacant hours, is the record of the onward march of Humanity towards an end. Where there is no belief in such an end, and therefore no advance towards it, no stirrings of a Divine Word in a people's bosom, where not as yet the beast's heart has been taken away, and a man's heart given, there History cannot be said to be. They belong not therefore to History, least of all to sacred History, those Babels, those cities of confusion, those huge pens, into which by force and fraud, the early hunters of men, the Nimrods and the Sesostrises drave, and compelled their fellows: and Scripture is only most true to its idea while it passes them almost or wholly in silence by, while it lingers rather on the plains of Mamre with the man that "believed God and it was counted unto him for righteousness" than by "populous No" or great Babylon, where no faith existed but in the blind powers of nature, and the brute forces of the natural man.

TRENCH'S HULSEAN LECTURE, ·

The Unity of Scripture.

WE have known hitherto in this country so little of the actual realities of war on a grand scale, that many are beginning to look upon the violent opposition to the government, and the slowness of the progress of our arms, as signs of hopeless discouragement. History, however, shows us that these are·the inevitable incidents of all wars waged by a free people. This might be abundantly illustrated by many remarkable events in English history, from the days of the Great Rebellion down through the campaigns of the Prince of Orange, and of Marlborough, to the wars which grew out of the events of the French Revolution. War is always entered upon amidst a vast deal of popular enthusiasm, which is utterly unreasoning. It is the universal voice of history, that such enthusiasm is wholly unreliable in supporting the prolonged and manifold burdens which are inseparable from every war waged on an extensive scale, and for a long period. The popular idea of war is a speedy and decisive victory, and an immediate occupation of the enemy's capital, followed by a treaty of peace by which the objects of the war are permanently secured. Nothing is revealed to the excited passions of the multitude, but dazzling visions of national glory, purchased by small privations, and the early and complete subjugation of their enemies. It is, therefore, not unnatural that at the first reverse they should yield at once to an unmanly depression, and, giving up all for lost, they should vent upon the government for its conduct of the war, and upon the army and its generals for their failure to make their dreams of victory realities, an abuse as unreasoning as was their original enthusiasm.

Experience has taught the English people that the progress of a war never fulfils the popular expectations; that although victory may be assured at last to patient and untiring vigor and energy in its prosecution, yet during the continuance of a long war there can be no well-founded hope of a uniform and constant series of brilliant triumphs in the field, illustrating the profound wisdom of the policy of the Cabinet; that, on the contrary, all war, even that which is most successful in the end. consists rather in checkered fortunes, of alternations of victory and disaster, and that its conduct is generally marked by what were evidently, when viewed in the light of experience, blunders so glaring in the policy adopted by the government, or in the strategy of its generals, that the wonder is success was achieved at all. The

English have thus been taught that the true charac-
teristic of public opinion in its judgment of a war
should be, not hopefulness or impatience of immediate
results, but rather a stern endurance—that King-
quality of heroic constancy which, rooted deep in a
profound conviction of the justice of the cause, sup-
ports a lofty public spirit equally well in the midst of
temporary disaster and in the hour of assured triumph.

We have had no such experience here. Our people are perhaps more easily excited by success, and
more readily depressed by reverses, than the English,
and it is, therefore, worth while to consider how they
carried on war on a grand scale and for a protracted
period. It will be found, if we mistake not, that the
denunciations of the government, so common among
us of late, and the complaints of the inactivity of
the army, have their exact counterpart in the history
of the progress of all the wars in which England has
been engaged since the days of the Great Rebellion.
He who draws consolation from the lessons of the
past, will not, we think, seek comfort in vain when
he discovers that in all those wars in which the government and the army have been so bitterly assailed
(except that of the American Revolution), England
has at last been triumphant. It is worth while then
to look into English history to understand how war
is successfully carried on notwithstanding the obstacles which, owing to a perverted public opinion, exist
within the nation itself. These difficulties, although

they inhere in the very nature of a free government, often prove, as we shall see, more fruitful of embarrassment to the favorable prosecution of a war than the active operations of the enemy.

We propose to illustrate the propositions which we have advanced by a study of the series of campaigns known in English history as the Peninsular War. We select this particular war because we think that in many of its events and in the policy which sustained it, there are to be observed many important, almost startling, parallelisms with our present struggle. We have, of course, no reference to any similarity existing in the principle which produced the two wars, but rather to the striking resemblance in the modes adopted by the two people for prosecuting war on a grand scale, and for the vindication of a principle regarded as of vital importance by them.

The Peninsular War on the part of England, as was contended by the ministry during its progress, and as is now universally recognized, was a struggle not only to maintain her commercial supremacy (which was then, as it is now, her life), but also to protect her own soil from invasion by the French, by transferring the scene of conflict to distant Spain. The general purpose of assisting the alliance against Napoleon seems always to have been a subordinate motive. It is now admitted by all historians, that upon success in this war depended not only England's rank among nations, but her very existence as an independent people.

The war was carried on for more than five years, and on a scale, so far as the number of men and the extent of the military operations are concerned, until then wholly unattempted by England in her European wars. The result, as it need not be said, was not only to crown the British arms with the most brilliant and undying lustre, but also to retain permanently in their places the party whose only title to public favor was that they had carried on the war against the most serious obstacles and brought it to a successful termination. Thus was delayed, it may be remarked, for at least twenty years, the adoption of those measures of reform which at last gave to England that place in modern civilization which had long before been reached by most of the nations of the Continent by passing through the trials of a bloody revolution. If we, then, in our dark hours, are inclined to doubt and despondency as to the final result, let us not forget the ordeal through which England successfully passed. We shall find that, in the commencement, there was the same wild and unreasoning enthusiasm with which we are familiar; the same bitter abuse and denunciation of the government at the first reverses; the same impatient and ignorant criticism of military operations; the same factious and disloyal opposition on the part of a powerful party; the same discouragement and despondency at times on the part of the true and loyal; the same prophecies of the utter hopelessness of success; the same complaints of grievous and burdensome. taxation, and predictions of the utter financial ruin of the country; the same violent attacks upon the government for its arbitrary decrees, and particularly for the suspension of the writ of *habeas corpus;* the same difficulties arising from the inexperience of the army; and the same weakness on the part of the government in not boldly and energetically supporting the army in the field. These are some of the more striking parallelisms between the Peninsular War and our own struggle, which a slight sketch of the progress of that war will render very apparent.

The insurrection in Spain which followed immediately upon a knowledge of the intrigues of Napoleon at Bayonne in April, 1807, by which the royal family was entrapped into an abdication of its right to the throne, and Joseph Bonaparte made king of that country, roused universal admiration and enthusiasm in England. It was thought by all parties that an obstacle to the further progress of Napoleon's schemes of the most formidable character had at last been found. It was the first popular insurrection in any country against Napoleon's power, and consequently, when the deputies from the Asturias reached England imploring succor, their appeals excited the popular feeling to the highest pitch, and the opposite parties in Parliament and the country vied with each other in demanding that England should aid the insurrection with the whole of her military power. It is curious to observe, that when the question of aid was brought before Parliament, Mr. Canning and Mr. Sheridan, who had probably never acted together before on any political question, rivalled each other in their praise of the Spaniards, and in their expressions of hope and belief that Napoleon had at last taken a step which would speedily prove fatal to him. Large supplies were voted by acclamation, and an important expedition, afterwards operating in two columns, one under the command of Sir John Moore, the other under that of Sir Arthur Wellesley, was dispatched to the Peninsula to aid the insurgents. It is not our purpose to trace the progress of this expedition, but merely to notice the effect which its immediate results, the retreat to Corunna, and the Convention of Cintra, produced upon popular feeling in England. As we look back on the history of that time, the folly and madness which seized upon the popular mind when the terms of the Convention of Cintra became known, can only be explained by recalling the high-wrought and extravagant expectations of immediate success with which the war had been entered upon. By this Convention, and as the result of a single battle, Portugal was wholly evacuated by the French; yet such were the unreasonable demands of public opinion, that because the whole French army had not been made prisoners of war, the Ministry was almost swept away by the outburst, and it could only control the storm by removing the

two generals highest in rank. It required all the
family and political influence of the third, Sir Arthur
Wellesley, to enable him to retain his position in the
army. The disastrous retreat of Sir John Moore's
army to Corunna, and the easy triumphs of the French.
at that period throughout all Spain, plunged the English into despair. Going from one extreme to another,
men who, only three months before, had quarrelled
with the army in Portugal because it had not given
them the spectacle of a French marshal and twenty
thousand of his soldiers as prisoners of war at Spit-
head, now spoke openly of the folly of any attempt
at all on the part of England to resist the progress of
the French arms in the Peninsula. In Parliament
there was the usual lame apology for disaster, an
attempt to shift the responsibility from the Ministry
to the General in command; but the great fact, that
all their hopes had been disappointed still remained,
and after the explanations of the government the
general despondency became more gloomy than ever.
It is not difficult in the light of history to see where
the blame of failure should rest. Any one who is
disposed now to sneer and cavil at the shortcomings
of our own administration, to impute to it views short-
sighted and impracticable in their policy, and to blame
it for want of energy and vigor in the prosecution of
the war, has only to turn to Colonel Napier's account
of the stupid blunders of the English government, its
absurd and contradictory orders, its absolute ignorance

not only of the elementary principles of all war, but of the very nature of the country in which the army was to operate, and of the resources of the enemy, to be convinced that had its mode of carrying on hostilities, (which was the popular one,) been adopted, in six months not an English soldier would have remained in the Peninsula except as a prisoner of war. The history of this campaign contains important lessons for us; it shows conclusively that the immediate results of war are never equal to the public expectation, and that if this public expectation, defeated by the imbecility of the government, or soured by disaster in the field, is to be the sole rule by which military operations are to be judged, no war for the defence of a principle can long be carried on.

Fortunately for the fame and the power of England, the Ministry, although ignorant of the true mode of prosecuting hostilities, had sense enough to perceive that their only true policy was perseverance. They were strong enough to resist the formidable opposition which the events we have referred to developed in Parliament and the country, and, undismayed by the experience of the past, concluded a ·treaty with the Provisional Government of Spain, by which they pledged England never to abandon the national cause until the French were driven across the Pyrenees. The army was placed upon a better footing, was largely reinforced, and Sir Arthur Wellesley was appointed to the chief command. The government, not

yet wholly awakened from its illusions, still thought
it practicable to reach Madrid in a single campaign,
and to that end the efforts of Wellington were directed.   It became necessary first to dislodge Soult
at Oporto, and the magnificent victory of the English-
gained by the passage of the Douro at that point went
far to revive confidence at home in the invincibility
of their army.   Yet so clear is it that victory in war
often depends upon what, for some better name, we
may call mere good fortune, that we have the author-
ity of the Duke of Wellington himself for saying,
that this army, which had just exhibited such prodi-
gies of valor, was then in such a state of demoralization, that although "excellent on parade, excellent to
fight, it was worse than an enemy in a country, and
liable to dissolution alike by success or defeat."   Certainly no severer criticism has ever been justified by
the inexperience and want of discipline of our own
raw levies than that contained in this memorable de-
claration.   A little reflection and candor might perhaps teach us, as it did the English, that nothing can
compensate for the want of experience, and that every
allowance is to be made for disasters where it is
necessary to educate both officers and soldiers in the
actual presence of the enemy.   Wellington soon afterwards moved towards the Spanish frontier, hoping by
a junction with the army under Cuesta to fight a
battle with the French which would open to him the
road to the capital.   The battle was fought at Tala-

vera, and although it has since been claimed by the English as one of their proudest victories, and the name of TALAVERA is now inscribed upon the standards of the regiments who took part in it with those of Salamanca and Vittoria, yet the result was in the end, that Wellington was obliged to retreat to Lisbon just three months after he had set out from that place, having left his wounded in the hands of the French, having escaped as if by a miracle from being wholly cut off in his retreat, and having lost one-third of his army in battle and by disease. Of course the blame was thrown upon the want of co-operation on the part of the Spaniards. This we have nothing to do with; it is the result of the campaign with which we are concerned. Dependence upon the Spaniards was certainly, as it turned out, a fault, but it was one of the fair chances of war, and it was a fault in which Wellington, made wise by experience, was never again detected.

When the news of the untoward result of this campaign reached England, the clamor against the Government and against Wellington was quite as violent as that excited by the disasters of Sir John Moore's army. The opposition in Parliament took advantage of this feeling to rouse public opinion to such a manifestation as might compel the termination of the war in the Peninsula and drive the ministry from office. The Common Council of London, probably a fair exponent of the opinions of the middle

class, petitioned the King not to confirm the grant of
£2000 a year, which the Ministry had succeeded in
getting Parliament to vote to Wellington.   The peti-
tioners ridiculed the idea that a battle attended with
such results should be called a victory.   " It should
rather be called a *calamity*," they said, " since we were
obliged to seek safety in a precipitate flight, abandon-
ing many thousands of our wounded countrymen into
the hands of the French."   In the opinion of the strategists in the Common Council and of their friends in
Parliament, Wellington might be a brave officer, but he
was no general; he had neglected the protection of his
flanks and his line of communication.   When it is remembered, that at this very time, Wellington, profiting
by the experience of the past, was diligently making
his army really effective within the lines of Torres
Vedras, from which stronghold it was in due time to
sally forth like a giant refreshed, never to rest until
it had planted the English flag on the heights of
Toulouse, we may perhaps smile at the presumption
of those who, sincere well wishers to the cause, dis-
played only their ignorance in their criticism.   But
what shall be said of those who, knowing better, being
quite able to understand the wisdom of the policy
adopted by the General to insure success in the stu-
pendous enterprise in which the country was engaged,
yet with a factious spirit and with the sole object of
getting into power themselves, took advantage of the

excitement of the ignorant multitude to paralyze the
energies of the government?

That hideous moral leprosy, which seems to be the
sad but invariable attendant upon all political discussions in a free government, corrupting the very sources
of public life, breeding only the base spirit of faction, had taken complete possession of the opposition,
and in its sordid calculations, the dishonor of the
country, or the danger of the army, was as nothing provided the office, the power, and the patronage of the
government were secured in their hands. It mattered
little to them, provided they could drive the ministry
from office, whether its downfall was brought about by
blunders in Spain, or by the King's obstinacy about
Catholic Emancipation, or by an obscure quarrel
about the influence of the Lords of the bed-chamber.
The sincerity of these declamations of the opposition
was curiously enough put to the test some time afterwards, when the ministry, wearied by the factious
demagogueism with which all their measures were
assailed, and understanding perfectly their signifi-
cance, boldly challenged their opponents, if they were
in earnest, to make a definite motion in the House
of Commons, that Portugal should be abandoned to
its fate. This move completely unmasked their game,
and for a time silenced the clamor, for it was perfectly understood on all hands, that deep in the popular heart, undisturbed by the storms which swept over
its surface, there was a thorough and abiding convic-

tion of the absolute necessity of resisting the progress of Napoleon's arms, and that the real safety of England herself required that that resistance should then be made in Spain. Still this noisy clamor did immense mischief; it weakened the government, it prolonged the strife, it alarmed the timid, it discouraged the true, and it so far imposed upon Napoleon himself, that thinking that in these angry invectives against the government he found the real exponent of English sentiment, he concluded, not unnaturally, that the people were tired and disgusted with the war, and that the privations which it occasioned were like a cancer, slowly but surely eating out the sources of national life.

In the midst of these violent tumults at home, Wellington was silently preparing for his great work within the lines of Torres Vedras. It would not be easy to overrate the difficulties by which he was surrounded. He was fully aware of the outcry which had been raised against him; he knew that from a Cabinet so weakened by internal dissensions as to be on the verge of overthrow from the vigorous assaults of the opposition, and from its own unpopularity occasioned by the failure of the Walcheren expedition, and the disasters in the Peninsula, he could expect no thorough and reliable support. Indeed the government, almost in despair, threw the whole responsibility for the military measures on the Continent on him alone. He accepted the responsibility in a most magnanimous spirit. "I conceive," he writes, "that the honor and the interests of the country require that we should hold our position here as long as possible, and, please God, I will maintain it as long as I can. I will neither endeavor to shift from my own shoulders on those of the ministers, the responsibility for the failure, by calling for means which I know they cannot give, and which perhaps would not add materially to the facility of attaining our object; nor will I give to the ministers, who are not strong, and who must feel the delicacy of their own situation, an excuse for withdrawing the army from a position which, in my opinion, the honor and interest of the country require they should maintain as long as possible." Animated by this heroic sense of duty, the Commander-in-Chief prepared to contend against the 200,000 men under Massena, whom Napoleon had sent to chase him into the sea. He had, to oppose this immense force, only 25,000 English soldiers, and about the same number of Portuguese tolerably or-ganized. Secure within the lines of Torres Vedras, he quietly waited until the want of provisions, and the utter hopelessness of an assault upon his position forced upon Massena the necessity of retreating. Then instantly pursuing, in a series of battles, of almost daily occurrence, he drove Massena out of Portugal, and reached once more the Spanish frontier in May, 1811, nearly three years after the English had sent an army to the assistance of the Peninsula.

2

Here he rested for a long time, making prepara-
tions for the siege of Badajoz and Ciudad Rodrigo,
operations requiring time, and the success of which
was essential to the safety of the army in its further
progress.   Still, so little was Wellington's position,
military and political, understood in England even at
that time, after all the proofs he had given of consum-
mate ability, that public clamor was again roused
against the mode adopted by him for conducting the
war.   As there were no disasters at which to grumble,
people talked of "barren victories," because, like
those of Crecy and Azincourt, they brought no terri-
torial acquisitions, forgetting then what they have
never been weary of boastingly proclaiming since,
that these victories were the best proofs that their
army was distinguished by the highest military qualities, which, properly directed and supported, were
capable of achieving the most glorious results.   So
profound was the conviction of the immense superiority of the French both in numbers, and in the
quality of their troops, that the public mind was in a
state of feverish anxiety, and many of the stoutest
hearts gave way to despair.   About this period Sir
Walter Scott writes to Mr. Ellis: "These cursed,
double cursed news (from Spain) have sunk my spirits
so much, that I am almost at disbelieving a Providence; God forgive me, but I think some evil demon
has been permitted in the shape of this tyrannical
monster, whom God has sent on the nations visited

in his anger. The spring-tide may, for aught I know, break upon *us* in the next session of Parliament. There is an evil fate upon us in all we do at home or abroad." So Sir James Mackintosh, writing to Gentz, at Vienna: "I believe, like you, in a resurrection, because I believe in the immortality of civilization, but when, and by whom, and in what form, are questions which I have not the sagacity to answer, and on which it would be boldness to hazard a conjecture. A dark and stormy night, a black series of ages may be prepared for our posterity, before the dawn that opens the more perfect day. Who can tell how long that fearful night may be before the dawn of a brighter morrow? The race of man may reach the promised land; but there is no assurance that the present generation will not perish in the wilderness." As if to render the situation more gloomy, if possible, the Marquis of Wellesley, the brother of Wellington, left the ministry upon the avowed ground that the government would not support the war with sufficient vigor. History has stripped his conduct of any such worthy motive, and shown that the real trouble was his anxiety to supplant Mr. Perceval. At the same time the attack was kept up in the opposite quarter. "No man in his senses," said Sir Francis Burdett, "could entertain a hope of the final success of our arms in the Peninsula. Our laurels were great but barren, and our victories in their effects mere defeats." Mr. Whitbread, too, as

usual, was not behindhand with his prophecies. " He
saw no reason," he said, " to alter his views respecting
peace ; war must otherwise terminate in the subjugation of either of the contending powers. They were
both great ; but this was a country of factitious greatness ; France was a country of natural greatness."
So, General Tarleton " had the doctrine of Mr. Fox
in his favor, who wished for the pencil of a Cervantes
to be able to ridicule those who desired to enter upon
a continental war."*

Thus, from universal enthusiasm in favor of the

---

* The following description of the opposition of that day, taken from
the *Annual Register* for 1812, bears so striking a likeness to the pecu-
liarities of the leaders of an insignificant, but restless faction among us,
that, omitting the old-fashioned drapery of the proper names, they seem
to have sat for the photograph. "It may be remarked as a most singu-
lar circumstance, that those persons in this country who profess to have
the greatest abhorrence of ministerial tyranny and oppression, look with
the utmost coolness on the tyranny and oppression of Bonaparte. .The
regular opposition do not mention it with that abhorrence which might
be expected from them ; but the leaders of the popular party in Parliament go further. They are almost always ready to find an excuse for
the conduct of Bonaparte. The most violent and unjustifiable acts of
his tyranny raise but feeble indignation in their minds, while the most
trifling act of ministerial oppression is inveighed against with the utmost
bitterness. Ready and unsuspecting credence is given to every account
of Bonaparte's success; while the accounts of the success of his opponents are received with coldness and distrust. Were it not for these
things, the conduct of Mr. Whitbread and his friends would be hailed
with more satisfaction, and inspire more confidence with the real lovers
of their country ; for they deserve ample credit for the undaunted and
unwearied firmness with which they have set themselves against abuses
and against every instance of oppression."

Spanish war, public opinion, at first manifesting itself
through the factious spirit of the opposition, at length
spoke through all its organs, in tones of despondency
and despair, of the situation and prospects of the
country, and simply because there had not been that
sort of military success which it could understand, to
sustain and direct it. Universal distrust seized upon
the public mind, and had it not been for the heroic
constancy of that great Commander, whose task in
supporting the ministry at home was at least as difficult as that of beating the French in Spain, the glory
of England had sunk forever.

Yet it happened, as it so often happens in the order
of Divine Providence, in the moral as in the physical
world, that the night was darkest just before dawn.
Amidst all this universal despondency and sinister
foreboding, events were preparing which in a few
short months changed the whole face of Europe, and
forced back that torrent of revolutionary success which
had spread over the whole Continent, until it over-
whelmed the country where it had its source in complete ruin. The discussions in Parliament to which
we have referred took place in February, 1812.
With the siege of Ciudad Rodrigo on the eighteenth
of January of that year, with the fall of Badajoz on
the 26th of March, the first battle of Salamanca on
the 20th of July, and Napoleon's invasion of Russia
in June in the same year, began the downfall of the
French Empire.

Wellington at last reached Madrid in August, 1812, more than four years later than he ought to have done, according to the strategists of Parliament and the Press. This was all forgotten at the moment, so magic a wand is held by success. The fickle voice of popular applause was again heard, echoing the spirit of confidence which his persistent and undaunted conduct had revived in the hearts of his countrymen. His career of victory, however, was destined not to be unchecked, and when, after his occupation of Madrid, his unsuccessful assault upon the Castle of Burgos rendered a retreat to the Portuguese frontier and the evacuation of the capital a proper military movement, although that retreat was compensated for by the abandonment of Andalusia by the French, in order to concentrate their whole force against him, still the blind multitude could not be made to understand it, and began again to murmur.

It is not now difficult to see that the victory at Salamanca was really what the far-seeing sagacity of Marshal Soult predicted at the time it would become, "a prodigious historical event," that it was the pivot on which at that time hinged the destinies of England, one of those battles of which we see perhaps a dozen only in the whole course of History which are really decisive of the fate of Empires. It completely unloosed the French power in the Peninsula, and prepared the way for the great success of Vittoria, the next year, which gave the *coup de grace* to the French military occupation of Spain. It is not our present purpose to trace the history of the next campaign, but it is curious to observe the effects produced by assured success upon that public opinion which had shifted so often and so strangely during the progress of this eventful struggle. The opposition, as their only hope of escape from political annihilation, and thinking to swim with the popular current, abused the ministers for not supporting Wellington with sufficient earnestness, complaining that they had taken the advice which they themselves had so often and so eloquently tendered. But it was of no avail; this wretched charlatanism was too transparent to impose upon any one, and of the great party who opposed the war, no one ever after rose to office or power in England. It required a whole, generation in the opinion of the English constituencies, to expiate the faults of those who had sneered at the great Duke, and had called the glorious fields of Vimeiro, Busaco, Talavera, Fuentes d'Onor, Ciudad Rodrigo, and Badajoz, names which had become associated with the proudest recollections of English renown, " mere barren victories, equal in their effects to defeats."

We pass now to the consideration of another class of difficulties inherent in the prosecution of every war, and generally of far greater magnitude than any other,—those connected with the raising of the vast sums of money required for the support of military

operations. In this important matter, if we mistake
not, there are some striking points of resemblance
between the English experience during the war, and
our present situation. It is the fashion among many
who seek to excite the public alarm on this subject
from unworthy, and sometimes, it may be feared, from
treasonable motives, to represent the enormous outlay
of the nation's wealth which is poured out to save the
nation's life, as wholly unparalleled in history. Yet
it may be asserted, without any fear of contradiction,
that England, with a population then little more than
half of that which now inhabits our loyal States, with
resources infinitely less in proportion at that time
than our own, her manufacturing industry so far as
external outlet was concerned wholly crippled by the
operation of the French continental system and her
own Orders in Council, expended, during every
year of the Peninsular war, as large a sum as has
been required here each year to create and keep up
the gigantic force now in arms to put down the Rebellion. During the five years that the war lasted,
her average annual expenditure exceeded ninety
millions of pounds sterling or four hundred and fifty
millions of dollars, which is about the same sum
which is demanded of us. No one, of course, pretends
to say that this rate of expenditure is not appalling,
yet it concerns us to know that it is not unprecedented,
and that these vast amounts have been raised from
national resources far inferior to our own. It should

not be forgotten, also, that they represent the money price of England's independence, and if ours is secured by a far greater outlay, we certainly are not disposed to quarrel with the wisdom of the investment.

The question is, how were these immense sums raised in England? The man who would have predicted, at the commencement of the war with France, that the English national debt would at its close exceed one thousand millions of pounds sterling, and that the country would be able to bear such a burden, would have been regarded as a visionary as wild as he who in this country, two years ago, might have foretold the present amount of our national debt, and have contended that, in spite of it, the public credit would remain unimpaired. The difficulty in England of raising these vast sums was tenfold greater than it is here. Napoleon, looking upon England as the Southern people have been taught to regard us, as a purely commercial nation, undoubtedly placed more reliance for ultimate success upon the instinct of money getting, which would shrink from the pecuniary sacrifices necessary in a prolonged struggle, than upon the mere victories of his army. Hence he pursued, during his whole career, an inflexible purpose of ruining English Commerce, and by a series of measures known as the Continental system, endeavored to exclude English ships and English products from the markets of the world. The effect of these measures, although not so serious as he wished and had anticipated, nevertheless crippled enormously the resources of England just at the period when they were most needed.

Taking the three years before the issuing of the Orders in Council and the vigorous enforcement of the Continental system, which were coincident in point of time with the commencement of the Spanish war, the average annual exports sank from fifty-seven millions to twenty-three millions, taking the average of three years after they had been in operation. Taxes were laid on at a most burdensome rate. The income tax was ten per cent., and besides, specific war taxes amounting to more than twenty millions a year were imposed. Notwithstanding all these taxes, the debt increased more than one thousand millions of dollars during the Peninsular war. Discontent and violence among the laboring classes became universal, and it was remarked that the achievement of the greatest victories in Spain was celebrated in England "amidst a population who had been prevented by the burden of taxation on the absolute necessaries of life, from securing a livelihood by the strictest industry, and thus pauperism had been generated throughout the land, a pauperism aggravated by a spirit of pillage, which it required a strong military force to repress." Bankruptcy and ruin fell upon the trading classes, and absolute exhaustion of the resources of the country seemed almost reached. The public stocks had sunk to such a degree that the

three per cents., which are now always above 90 per
cent., were rarely higher during the war than 65 per
cent., and so depressed at last had the public credit
become, that the last loan of the Continental war, that
of April, 1815, was taken by the Contractor at 53 per
cent., and paid for in the depreciated paper of the
day, and yet the Chancellor of the Exchequer was
congratulated even by the opposition for having made
" a good operation." The Bank was in a state of
chronic suspension, the buying and selling of gold were
prohibited to the public under severe penalties, and
yet every gold guinea which was sent by the Government to the army in Spain (and nothing else would
answer the purpose of money in that country) cost
thirty per cent. premium. How England survived
all this complication of troubles is one of the mar-
vels of history, but it is not our purpose to discuss
that question. The great fact that the money required
was raised somehow is all we have to do with at present. When we have been at war for twenty years,
and are forced, in order to raise the means of carrying
it on, to submit to one tithe of the sacrifices which
were endured by the English, we may then perhaps
begin seriously to consider the money value of the
Union.

The lesson which this review of the progress of
the Peninsular war teaches, is, it seems to us, one of
hope and encouragement, for if it shows anything
it proves clearly, that in the support of public

opinion, and in the means requisite to maintain a great army, those fundamental essentials of real military success, our Government is immeasurably stronger than the English ever was at any period of the war. It teaches also another important lesson, and that is, that there is such a thing as public opinion falsely so called, which is noisy just in proportion as its real influence is narrow and restricted. One of the most difficult and delicate tasks of the statesman is to distinguish the true from this false opinion, the factious demagogue from the grumbling but sincere patriot, and to recognize with a ready instinct the voice which comes from the depths of the great heart of the people, in warning it may be sometimes, in encouragement often, but always echoing its abiding faith in the ultimate triumph of the good cause.

We have confined ourselves in our illustrations to the discussion of questions as they affected the success of purely military operations, because we feel that *here* our grand business is to clear away the obstacles, real or fancied, which may in any way impair our military efficiency. In military success alone, we are firmly convinced, is to be found the true solution of our whole difficulty, the only force which can give vitality or permanence to any theory of settlement. As the matter now stands, it is idle to hope for either peace or safety until this question of military superiority is unmistakably and definitively settled. Upon this point then, the increase of our military efficiency,

which embraces not merely the improvement of the
condition of the army, but also, as we have endeavored to show by English examples, and in a greater
degree than is often supposed, the support of the
Government in its general policy of conducting the
war, should the efforts of all those who influence
public opinion be concentrated.

There is a certain class of men among us, not very
numerous, perhaps, but still, owing to their position
and culture, of considerable influence, who, accus-
tomed to find in the European armies their standard
of military efficiency, are disposed to doubt whether a
force, composed as ours is of totally different materials,
can accomplish great results. We may admit at once
the superiority of foreign military organization, the
result of the traditions of centuries of military experience, digested into a thorough system, and carried out
by long trained officers perfectly versed in the details
of the service. Much inconvenience has necessarily
resulted in our case from the ignorance of Regimental
Officers, to a greater degree probably, however, from a
want of proper care and attention on their part to the
troops when in camp, than from any gross incompetency or misconduct on the field of battle. Instances
of such misconduct there have undoubtedly been, but,
considering the number of the officers and their want
of experience, those instances are extremely rare, and
when we call to mind the number of officers who have
fallen, while leading their men in battle, out of pro-

portion, as it undoubtedly is, with the losses in other
war we may well palliate deficiencies in this respect,
out of considerations for their heroic gallantry and de-
votion. We do not underrate certainly the value of
good officers, but history tells us that great victories
have been achieved by armies who were no better led
than ours. The incompetency of his officers was one of
Wellington's standing complaints in Spain. Most of
them knew absolutely nothing beyond the mere routine
of garrison duty; they were all what is technically
called "gentlemen," for each one had purchased his
commission at a high price, but they had had no sys-
tematic training in military schools, nearly all of them
had had no actual experience of war, and their average
intelligence was undoubtedly below that of the men
who hold similar positions in our army.* All accounts agree that at that period, the scientific branches

---

* We have no room to enumerate in detail the complaints made by
the Duke of the officers of his army. Those who are interested in the
subject may consult Col. Gurwood's 4th volume, pages 343, 346, 352,
363, 385, 399, and 407. The whole story is summed up, however, in
the general order occasioned by the disorderly retreat from Burgos, in
which the Duke said " that discipline had deteriorated during the campaign in a greater degree than he had ever witnessed, or ever read of in
any army, and this, without any disaster, or any unusual privation or
hardship; that the officers had from the first lost all command over
their men, and that the true cause of this unhappy state of affairs was
to be found *in the habitual neglect of duty by the Regimental Officers.*"
This is the army of which the Duke said later, that "with it, he could go
anywhere and do anything." and, good or bad, it saved Europe—in the
English sense.

of the great art of war were almost wholly neglected
in the British army, and such was the happy ignorance of the elements of strategy, that at a court
martial composed of general officers for the trial of
General Whitelock in 1808, for his failure at Buenos
Ayres, it was necessary to explain to the court what
was meant in military phrase by the " right bank " of
a river.

It is said again, by those who have the standard of
foreign armies always before their eyes, that among
our soldiers there is not a proper deference to rank,
too much *camaraderie* in short, and that this is fatal
to discipline. But it should be remembered that
mere formal discipline may be one thing, and the true
spirit of discipline another, and yet both may answer
the same purpose. The first may be more showy
than the latter, but not more valuable to real military
efficiency. Everything depends upon the character
of the soldier who is to be governed by it. The British army is composed, as we all know, of the refuse
of the population, and in the war in the Peninsula it
was largely reinforced by the introduction into its
ranks of convicts taken from the hulks, who were
there expiating infamous offences. With such men,
motives based on a sense of duty were powerless.
Drunkenness, theft, marauding, a mutinous spirit under privations, and a fierce thirst of license which
defied all control in the hour of victory, these were
the brutal passions which could only be checked by

the equally brute hand of force. But from such a
vile herd, made useful only as a slave is made useful,
by fear of the lash, to the civilized, sober, well educated American citizen, animated with the conscious-
ness that he is fighting for a great cause, in the success
of which he and his children have a deep personal
interest, and who learns obedience because both his
common sense and his sense of duty recognize its
necessity, how immeasurable is the distance! The
American volunteer, in this respect, has not had justice done to his excellence.   He is certainly a soldier
essentially *sui generis,* and when we hear sneers at
his want of discipline, let us remember that although
he may not regard his officers as superior beings, yet
experience has already shown that in the cheerful per-
formance of his new duties under privations; in his
freedom from those vices which in many minds are
inseparably associated with the very idea of a soldier;
in his courage, endurance, and steadiness in battle;
and more than all, in those higher qualities which are
the fruit of his education, general intelligence, and
love of country, he presents himself to us as a figure
hitherto wholly unknown in military history.

One of the most cruel statements which party ran-
cor has circulated in regard to the condition of the
army is, that the rate of sickness and mortality is
excessive, and that this is due to the neglect of the
government. Fortunately we have the means of show-
ing that these statements are false. From June 1,

1861, to March 1, 1862—nine months—the annual rate of mortality for the whole army is ascertained to be 53 in a thousand, and the sickness rate 104 in a thousand. The returns for the summer campaigns are not yet printed, but it will appear from them that in the army of the Potomac on the 10th of June, after the battle of Fair Oaks, and while the army was encamped on the Chickahominy, the whole number of sick, present and absent, compared with the whole force of that army present and absent, was 128 in a thousand. During the stay of the army on the Peninsula it lost less than 14,000 men by death from disease and wounds, and the average sickness rate during the campaign was about that which has for some time prevailed in the whole army, less than ten per cent. of the whole force. It appears, strange to say, that the army was more healthy when in the trenches before Yorktown, than at any other period of the campaign. Compare this with the English experience. We have already said that Wellington lost about one-third of his whole army from malarious fever on his retreat from Talavera: on the 1st October, 1811, the Anglo-Portuguese army had 56,000 men fit for duty, and 23,000 sick in hospitals; and in the Crimea, while the annual rate of mortality for the whole war was 232 in a thousand, the period of active operations, the last three months of 1854 and the first three months of 1855, shows the fearful rate of 711 deaths in every thousand men.

3

It cannot be doubted that to many the most unfavorable symptom of our present condition is the slow progress of our arms. This slowness is more apparent than real, for the history of modern warfare scarcely shows an instance in which so great real progress has been made in the same space of time, and it is manifest that whenever our northern soldiers have had a chance of fighting the enemy on anything like equal terms, they have fully maintained their superiority. It is none the less true, however, that public expectation in this matter has been much disappointed, and it is curious to look at some of the explanations given for it. The Prince de Joinville, in his recent pamphlet, speaking of the battle of Fair Oaks and of the neglect to throw bridges over the Chickahominy at the proper time, by means of which the whole rebel army might have been taken in flank, and probably destroyed, ascribes the neglect on one page to what he calls *la lenteur Américaine*, which he seems to think always leads our countrymen to let the chance slip of doing the right thing at the right time, and again on the next to "*faute d'organisation, faute de hiérarchie, faute de lien, qui en resulte entre l'âme du chef et l'armée, lien puissant qui permet à un General de demander à ses soldats et d'en obtenir aveuglement ces efforts extraordinaires qui gagnent les battailles.*" In other words, General M'Clellan, knowing that he could gain a decisive victory by laying down half a dozen bridges, which, it is stated, were all ready for the purpose, actually refused to order his soldiers to do it, because he was afraid they would not obey his orders. And this is the Prince's judgment of an army, which, a few weeks later, according to his own account, fought five battles in as many days, all, with one exception, victories over an enemy at least double its numbers, and arrived at its new base on the James River in excellent condition and without the slightest taint of demoralization. This illustration shows the absurdity of ascribing the want of immediate success to *la lenteur Américaine*, a quality, by the way, which we learn for the first time is one of our national characteristics.

Among the many causes which might be named, all perfectly legitimate, and presenting no obstacle which a little experience will not remove, we venture to suggest but one, and that is the character of the early military education of our higher officers. The system pursued at West Point, although admirable for qualifying officers for the scientific and staff corps of the army, seems to fail in teaching the young soldier, what is just now the most important quality he can possess for command, the character and capacity of volunteer soldiers. The system of discipline he has been taught is that which governs the regular army, a system modelled upon the English, which is, with the exception of that in use in Russia, the most brutal and demoralizing known in any army in Europe. No wonder, therefore, that when our educated

soldiers are suddenly placed in high positions, and
with great responsibilities, and when they discover
that the sort of discipline which they have been
taught is wholly out of place in securing the efficiency
of a volunteer army, they are led to doubt whether it
can ever be made efficient at all. These prejudices,
however, are wearing away before the test of actual
experience. Generals are gradually learning that
they may confide in their men, even for desperate
undertakings; they begin to see in their true light
the many admirable qualities of the volunteer; and
he, in turn, begins to understand something of that
military system which seemed at first so irksome and
meaningless to him; and the advance of the army in
the essentials of discipline has been proportionably
rapid.

There is a good deal of talk about the impossibility
of conquering or subjugating the South, which is
based upon very vague notions of what conquest and
subjugation signify. It is surprising to find how even
intelligent men have been imposed upon by this fa-
vorite boast of the rebels and their sympathizers. A
pretended saying of Napoleon is quoted, that "it is
impossible to prevent any people determined on
achieving its independence, from accomplishing its
purpose;" and it is confidently asked whether any one
ever heard of the subjugation of twelve millions of
people determined to be free. We reply that history,
ancient and modern, is full of instances of the only

sort of conquest or subjugation which any sane man
proposes shall be submitted to by the South. No one
thinks it possible or necessary, for the purpose in view,
to occupy the whole South with garrisons, but simply
to destroy the only support upon which its arrogant
pretensions are based, namely, its military power.
This gone, what becomes of all the rest? and this
remaining, where is there any hope of permanent
peace and safety to us? For what is all war but an
appeal to force to settle questions of national interest
which peaceful discussion has failed to settle; and
what is an army, but only another argument, the
ultima ratio, which, if successful in decisive battles,
must give the law to the conquered? To say nothing
of instances in ancient history, Poland, Hungary, and
Lombardy in our day were just as determined to be
free as the South is, and quite as full of martial ardor ;
and certainly Prussia, Spain under the Bonaparte
dynasty, and the French Empire, are all examples of
nations which valued their independence, and had
tenfold the resources for maintaining it which the
South possesses ; yet the capture of Warsaw, the sur-
render of Villagos, the battles of Novara, of Jena, of
Salamanca, and of Waterloo respectively, settled as
definitively the fate of the inhabitants of those coun-
tries and their future condition as if the terms imposed
by the conquering army had been freely and unani-
mously agreed upon by the representatives of the
people in Congress assembled. And, in like manner,

can any one doubt, looking at the present comparative
resources of the two sections, that if we should gain
two decisive battles, one in the East and the other in
the West, which should result in the total disorgani-
zation of the two rebel armies, and thus enable us
to interpose an impassable barrier between them, we
should soon hear a voice imploring in unmistakable
accents peace on our own terms? It would not be a
matter of choice, but of necessity; a simple question
of how far the progress of exhaustion had been carried, and that once settled, and no reasonable hope of
success remaining, the war would not last a week
longer. This is the experience of all nations, and our
Southern rebels, notwithstanding their noisy boast-
ing, do not differ in their capacity of resistance
from the rest of mankind. "Hard pounding this,
gentlemen," said the Duke of Wellington to his
officers, as he threw himself within one of the un-
broken squares of his heroic infantry at Waterloo,
"*but we'll see who can pound the longest;*" and the
ability of that infantry to "pound the longest" on
that day settled the fate of Europe for generations.

Let us bend, then, our united energies to secure,
as much as in us lies, success in the field, and that
success gained, we may be sure that all things will
follow. Let us recognize with confidence as co-workers
in this great object all, never mind what opinions
they may entertain about the causes of the war, and
the new issues which its progress has developed, who

desire in all sincerity, no matter from what motive, the success of our arms. Upon such a basis, the wider and more catholic our faith becomes the better. "In essentials Unity; in non-essentials Liberty; in all things Charity:" this should be our motto. The only possible hope for the South is in our own divisions. Let us remember that with success all things are possible; without it, all our hopes and theories vanish into thin air. With success in the field, we should not only disarm the rebellion, and rid ourselves forever of the pestilent tribe of domestic traitors by burying them deep in that political oblivion which covers the Tories of the Revolution, and those who sneered at the gallant exploits of our navy in the war of 1812, but also force public opinion abroad, whose faithlessness to the great principles which underlie all modern civilization has been one of the saddest developments of this sad war, to exclaim at last, "*Invidiam gloriâ superâsti.*"

www.ingramcontent.com/pod-product-compliance
Lightning Source LLC
Chambersburg PA
CBHW021450090426
42739CB00009B/1698